Tractors

Lori Dittmer

seedlings

CREATIVE EDUCATION • CREATIVE PAPERBACKS

Published by Creative Education and Creative Paperbacks
P.O. Box 227, Mankato, Minnesota 56002
Creative Education and Creative Paperbacks
are imprints of The Creative Company
www.thecreativecompany.us

Design by Ellen Huber; production by Chelsey Luther
Art direction by Rita Marshall
Printed in the United States of America

Photographs by Dreamstime (Hamiza Bakirci, Orangeline), Getty Images (Avalon_Studio, James Brey, Rick Dalton), iStockphoto (filonmar, mladn61, santosha, Veremeev), Shutterstock (Africa Studio, DeshaCAM, Luis Louro, Rihardzz, smereka, tuulijumala, Valentin Valkov)

Copyright © 2018 Creative Education, Creative Paperbacks
International copyright reserved in all countries. No part of this book may be reproduced in any form without written permission from the publisher.

Library of Congress Cataloging-in-Publication Data
Names: Dittmer, Lori, author.
Title: Tractors / Lori Dittmer.
Series: Seedlings.
Includes bibliographical references and index
Summary: A kindergarten-level introduction to tractors, covering their purpose, parts, role in farming, and such defining features as their big tires.
Identifiers: ISBN 978-1-60818-912-0 (hardcover) / ISBN 978-1-62832-528-7 (pbk) / ISBN 978-1-56660-964-7 (eBook)
This title has been submitted for CIP processing under LCCN 2017940117.

CCSS: RI.K.1, 2, 3, 4, 5, 6, 7;
RI.1.1, 2, 3, 4, 5, 6, 7; RF.K.1, 3; RF.1.1

First Edition HC 9 8 7 6 5 4 3 2 1
First Edition PBK 9 8 7 6 5 4 3 2 1

TABLE OF CONTENTS

Hello, Tractors! 4

Powerful Pullers 6

In the Cab 8

Heavy Loads 10

Tall Tires 12

Good Grip 14

What Do Tractors Do? 16

Goodbye, Tractors! 18

Picture a Tractor 20

Words to Know 22

Read More 23

Websites 23

Index 24

Hello, tractors!

Tractors are powerful farm machines.

They pull equipment across fields.

Farmers drive tractors. They sit in the cab. Some cabs are open. Closed cabs block the sun and wind.

Strong tractors can pull heavy loads.

They tow plows and balers. Tractors pull trailers, too. They take hay to farm animals.

Dual tractors have six or eight wheels.

Tractor tires are huge. Some are as tall as an adult!

Thick tire treads grip the ground. They help the tractor drive through muddy fields.

Tractors drive in all kinds of weather. They help farmers work in fields.

Picture a Tractor

20

Words to Know

balers: farm machines used to squeeze crops into bundles

trailers: vehicles that are pulled and carry something from one place to another

treads: ridges on a tire that make contact with the ground

Read More

Dieker, Wendy. *Tractors.*
Minneapolis: Jump!, 2013.

Nixon, James. *Tractors.*
Mankato, Minn.: Amicus, 2011.

Websites

Farm Safety for Just Kids
http://www.farmsafetyforjustkids.org
Learn how to be safe on farms, from tractors to grain bins.

Tractors for Children – Explore a Tractor with Blippi
https://www.youtube.com/watch?v=oR4vY9BEspQ
Watch a video to learn more about the parts of a tractor.

Note: Every effort has been made to ensure that the websites listed above are suitable for children, that they have educational value, and that they contain no inappropriate material. However, because of the nature of the Internet, it is impossible to guarantee that these sites will remain active indefinitely or that their contents will not be altered.

Index

animals 11
balers 11
cabs 8
farmers 8, 16
fields 7, 14, 16
plows 11
tires 13, 14
trailers 11
treads 14